STAND TALL
as TALL
as the TREES

How an Amazonian Community
Protected the Rain Forest

Patricia Gualinga and **Laura Resau**
Illustrated by **Vanessa Jaramillo**

Charlesbridge

SARAYAKU is my home.

It's deep in the rain forest of Ecuador.

My home is alive—

alive with trees towering, vines winding, and frogs singing.

Most of all, it's alive

with mystical beings who rule the forest—

the Amazanga.

They look human, but they're stronger,

and they protect the sacred forest

as they hide among trees and vines.

As rain *tap-tap-taps*,

my family kneels by the batán, making chicha.

Mamita tells tales in our language—Kichwa.

The tales warn,

"Do not mistreat the forest,

or the Amazanga will punish you."

I shut my eyes tight.
"Be brave, Paty," says Papito.
"Show respect,
and the forest will give you strength."

Papito is a wise yachak—
a shaman with one foot in this world
and one in the spirit world.

Mamita is the wise daughter of a yachak.

Be brave, Paty.

Papito's words echo as I sit in school.

Maybe learning can make me strong.

Knowing the world outside my forest

might give me power inside it.

So I leave my
humming, thrumming home
to study at high school in the smoking, roaring city.
Through years of trials and sorrows,
I find strength in the forest of my heart.

My diploma is a magic charm
that gives me a voice on the radio.
I spread our Kichwa tales—
the ones Mamita told by the batán—
tales that bring our pueblos together.

But then one day,
news comes from Sarayaku.
Men have invaded our land.
They bury dynamite
all around our forest home
to search for oil. BOOM, BOOM, BOOM!

The animals are dying.
The plants are dying.
And the Amazanga *wail!*

CHOP, CHOP, CHOP!

More men come

with helicopters and guns, shouts and uniforms,

fists and fire, orders and papers.

They say the government of Ecuador

sold the earth beneath our sacred forest—

sold it to an oil company.

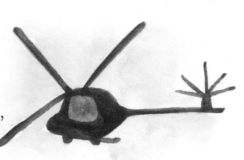

No one asked us first.

These men do not understand that our life and strength

come from the forest, from the beings within it.

They do not care that

our forest is *alive*.

My people know that I have one foot in the city
and one in the forest.
I'm part of two worlds, like the yachak.
"We need you, Paty," says my pueblo.

Inside my rainy green heart,
I hear Papito's voice: *Be brave, Paty*.
I hear the trees' song:
I will stand against mighty winds,
and all will see my flowers.
I hear the call: *We need you*.

So downstream I paddle,
back to the sacred forest.

Now it is barren.
Craters scorch the earth.
I see no vines winding,
no flowers blooming.
And no Amazanga.

Through tears, I search the land
till I find some parts still alive,
humming, thrumming with
insects and frogs.
Best of all—
I find the Amazanga!
With open arms I promise,
"We will protect you."

In turn, the forest gives us strength.
It brings together
the elders' deep wisdom,
the youths' new knowledge, and
the children's shining hope.

We gather—all of Sarayaku.
We dance and drum.
We sing songs, give speeches,
play flutes, paint faces,
wear beads, and don feathers.
We march and march and march.

With growing strength,

we travel the world to tell our story.

With growing hope,

we find lawyers and groups

who care about nature and culture.

With growing hearts,

we unite with other Indigenous peoples.

After years of hard work,
we make the oil company leave our land.
Juu-aaay! Hooray!

Still, we stand strong
to ensure that the Amazanga
will never again wail.
We fly to Costa Rica—
a group of women, men, children,
and even a tiny baby.

With hearts proud and hopeful,
we present our case to the
Court of Human Rights.

"Our sacred forest is alive," we explain.

"Without plants and animals, what will we eat?"

"Without clean rivers, what will we drink?"

The judges hear our speeches.

Maybe they hear the Amazanga's wails, too.

The court rules in our favor!
It orders the government of Ecuador
to make our forest safe again
and in the future to always ask first.

The government leaders agree.
Not only that, they also say,
"We're sorry."

Our Kichwa village sends a message to the world:
we have the right to protect our home.
When the forest breathes deeply,
the whole Earth breathes.

We need the forest
humming, thrumming
as it wends and winds,
sings and blooms.
It keeps us
all *alive*!

ABOUT THE KICHWA OF THE AMAZON RAIN FOREST

The Kichwa (also spelled Quichua) are a group of Indigenous, or Native, people in South America. The Kichwa language—spoken mainly in Ecuador and parts of Colombia and Peru—contains many dialects spoken by different communities within the Kichwa culture. Some Kichwa people live in the Andes Mountains, some on the coast, and some in the Amazon rain forest. Each group has adapted to a distinct environment and has a unique cultural identity.

In the Amazon, Kichwa people have traditionally depended on the rain forest for what they need to live. They carefully harvest wild plants to make their houses, baskets, dishes, and tools. Kichwa people usually travel by canoe or on foot. They plant vegetables such as starchy cassava (yuca) and gather fruits such as pineapple and papaya. They respectfully hunt for meat and use rivers for fishing, drinking, and bathing.

In recent years, some Kichwa people have brought outside conveniences into their lives, such as store-bought clothing and machine-made tools. Some Kichwa people study or work in larger towns, and many feel drawn back to the forest to gather strength. They seek a balance between modern technology and cultural traditions in order to stay connected with their ancestral land.

The Kichwa people feel that their community's health depends on a respectful relationship not only with plants and animals but also with mystical beings such as the Amazanga. Kichwa people believe that the Amazanga are powerful guardians and rulers of the old-growth rain forest. The Kichwa people of Sarayaku embrace "Kawsak Sacha" (the Living Forest), honoring the spirituality and ecology of the Amazon.

For several decades, the oil industry has threatened Kichwa communities through deforestation and pollution. Along with other Indigenous groups, Kichwa activists have raised their voices to protect their culture, well-being, and sacred forest. Paty—Patricia Gualinga, one of the authors of this book—and her home village of Sarayaku have been at the forefront of the movement, spreading the message of Kawsak Sacha far and wide.

Paty's community won an inspiring victory in 2012. The Inter-American Court of Human Rights, based in San José, Costa Rica, ruled in their favor against the government of Ecuador, which had permitted oil exploration without first consulting the Kichwa people. But there is still work to do. Promises and policies change with new presidents. Forest protectors must continue to pressure the Ecuadorian government—and the world—to respect the environment and Indigenous peoples' rights. Paty and her community are up for the challenge, and they encourage others to join them!

STANDING UP FOR LAND AROUND THE WORLD

Indigenous peoples across the globe have stood up for ancestral lands where they have lived for centuries or millennia. They are taking on challenges, such as discrimination, in order to honor and manage their sacred homelands with traditional, sustainable practices. Even after legal triumphs, Indigenous people keep working to strengthen their rights and ensure that governments uphold the laws that protect those rights. Here is a small sampling of the many Indigenous movements that have taken place around the world.

NORTH AMERICA

In British Columbia, Canada, First Nations people have fought for land rights for decades and have won important victories. In 2014 the Supreme Court of Canada gave the **Tsilhqot'in** (tsill-KO-tin) Nation the right to control 656 square miles (1,700 square kilometers) of ancestral land, including snow-topped mountains and lush pine forests. Although the Tsilhqot'in people don't have permanent settlements, they may still claim Indigenous use and management rights (called Aboriginal title in Canada) for land they use at least some of the time for activities such as hunting, fishing, and spiritual ceremonies. The law also says that the land cannot be developed, mined, drilled, or logged without this tribe's consent. The Canadian government may override the Aboriginal title only under special circumstances, after having meaningful consultations with the Tsilhqot'in Nation.

AFRICA

In the semiarid grasslands of Kenya and northern Tanzania, **Maasai** (mah-SY or MAH-sy) people work to protect their way of life. Traditionally the Maasai have moved seasonally with the cattle, sheep, and goats they graze. Since water is often scarce, the Maasai people migrate between wet-season and dry-season pastures—a sustainable practice. Although the Kenyan and Tanzanian governments have tried to force them to stay in one place, many Maasai have held on to their lifestyle. In recent years their culture has been threatened by developers, agriculture, corruption, and restricted land access to wildlife game reserves and national parks. Some Maasai people partner with organizations to protect their way of life on communal lands. In 2010 a new Kenyan constitution was created to ensure a more democratic system and protect human and environmental rights. Maasai and other Indigenous leaders helped draft this constitution, which strengthens Indigenous peoples' rights, respects cultural heritage, and protects ancestral lands.

EUROPE

For centuries the **Sámi** (SAH-mee) people have fished salmon and herded reindeer in the snowy northern regions that are now known as Norway, Finland, Sweden, and the Russian Kola Peninsula. For decades their traditional land has been threatened by oil exploration, mining, logging, dam building, and climate change. Historically, the Sámi people have faced oppression from governments and greater society. In Sweden and Finland, the Sámi languages were banned. In Norway, some Sámi groups lost rights to seasonally pasture reindeer there, due to national border policies with Sweden. In recent years, however, the Sámi people have made progress in protecting their culture and rights. Despite general bans on reindeer herding in Norway and Sweden, the Sámi people are permitted to continue this traditional practice. In a 2016 court case, a Sámi community in Sweden won rights to control hunting and fishing in the area.

ASIA

On the northern Japanese island of Hokkaido—amid majestic mountains, lakes, wetlands, and volcanoes—the Indigenous **Ainu** (AH-ee-noo) people have traditionally been hunter-gatherers and fishers. For centuries they spoke their own language and practiced nature-based spirituality. Over a hundred years ago, the Japanese government took Ainu land and forced the people to assimilate (adopt mainstream society's culture, language, religion, and more). The Ainu community began losing their traditions and language. Facing widespread discrimination, Ainu activists pressured the Japanese government to recognize and respect their culture, which resulted in the Ainu Cultural Promotion Law of 1997. In 2019 a new law, the Ainu Promotion Act, went a step further to actively support Ainu communities and take measures to stop discrimination. For example, now the Ainu people have the right to use national lands for traditional practices such as salmon fishing and sacred ceremonies.

OCEANIA

Aboriginal people have occupied the savanna of northern Australia for more than 50,000 years as hunter-gatherers. When Europeans colonized this land, mining and ranching threatened Aboriginal people's way of life. The community worked hard to get the Australian government to pass the Aboriginal Land Rights Act of 1976, which allowed them to reject development on their ancestral lands in the Northern Territory. In 1993, the historic Native Title Act recognized that Aboriginal people throughout Australia have rights to use and protect their ancestral land and water. Today many Aboriginal people work with conservation programs such as the Indigenous Ranger program and Indigenous Protected Areas program to care for their ecosystems. They use traditional fire management methods, protect threatened animal species, and safeguard sacred sites such as rocks, hills, and water holes.

GLOSSARY

Amazanga (ah-mah-ZAHN-gah): Mystical beings who, according to beliefs of the Kichwa people, are the supreme owners, guardians, and protectors of the sacred, old-growth Amazon rain forest. Kichwa people believe that the Amazanga are the most powerful of all the mystical beings in these woods.

batán (bah-TAHN): A large wooden container for making chicha.

chicha (CHEE-chah): A traditional South American drink made from root vegetables, grains, or fruit. Kichwa communities in the Amazon make chicha with cassava (also called yuca or manioc).

Inter-American Court of Human Rights: An independent court based in San José, Costa Rica, that hears legal cases and then rules whether a country has violated human rights. (There are other courts of human rights, such as the European Court of Human Rights.)

Ecuador: A South American country with Pacific coastal plains, the Andes Mountains, and the Amazon rain forest. Ecuador is home to many Kichwa communities as well as other Indigenous groups.

Kichwa (KEECH-wah): An Indigenous people who live in the Amazon rain forest of Ecuador; also their language. (Also spelled Quichua.)

pueblo (PWAY-bloh): The Spanish word for a village or town.

Sarayaku (sah-rah-YAH-koo): A village and territory near the Bobonaza River in the province of Pastaza in the Ecuadorian Amazon rain forest.

yachak (YAH-chahk): A shaman or traditional healer who is familiar with the spiritual and natural worlds.

For periodic updates on Indigenous land rights issues, please visit www.LauraResau.com/standastallasthetrees.

SELECTED SOURCES
(Listed by Indigenous Group)

KICHWA

Gonzalez, David. "At Home in the Jungle, Everything Is 'Alive and Has a Spirit.'" *New York Times*, April 20, 2018.

A photo-illustrated article that is easily found online and is written in a way that is accessible to young readers.

Gualinga, Eriberto, Mariano Machain, and David Whitbourn. *Children of the Jaguar*. Pueblo Originario Kichwa de Sarayaku and Amnesty International, 2012.

A thirty-minute film in Spanish with English subtitles, available on YouTube and created by the co-author's brother. (Look for Paty in the movie!)

TSILHQOT'IN

Fine, Sean. "Supreme Court Expands Land-Title Rights in Unanimous Ruling." *The Globe and Mail*, June 26, 2014.

Government of British Columbia website. "Tsilhqot'in Nation Declared Title Land."

Kids will probably need help reading these two articles, which are easily found online. Enjoy them together!

MAASAI

Myers Madeira, Erin. "Want to Save the Planet? Empower Women." *Global Program Lead for Indigenous Peoples and Local Communities*, Nature Conservancy, March 7, 2018.

This article is easily found online, and it includes a short video about empowering women in northern Tanzania.

Reynolds, Jan. *Only the Mountains Do Not Move: A Maasai Story of Culture and Conservation*. New York: Lee & Low Books, 2011.

A book for young readers.

SÁMI

Crouch, David. "Sweden's Indigenous Sámi People Win Rights Battle Against State." *Guardian*, February 3, 2016.

This article is easily found online.

Alatalo, Jaako. *Iina-Marja's Day: From Dawn to Dusk in Lapland*. Frances Lincoln Children's Books, 2011.

A book for young readers.

AINU

"Japan Prepares Law to Finally Recognize and Protect Its Indigenous Ainu People." *Washington Post*, February 15, 2019.

This article is easily found online.

Poisson, Barbara Aoki. *The Ainu of Japan*. Lerner Pub Group, 2002.

A book for young readers.

ABORIGINAL AUSTRALIANS

Colson, Mary. *Indigenous Australian Cultures*, Portsmouth, NH: Heinemann, 2012.

A book for young readers.

Nature Conservancy Australia website. "Working with Indigenous Australians for Conservation: Supporting Indigenous People to Manage Their Land for Conservation."

This article is easily found online and includes a video.

To my late father, my mother, my family, my husband, and my siblings, who gave me
deep knowledge and love of nature as humans' very life; also to the brave Pueblo of Sarayaku
who are building paths of struggle and dignity as a symbol and inspiration for future generations
—P. G.

To the Pueblo of Sarayaku, with my deepest gratitude and respect
—L. R.

With affection to all the children of the world, and especially to the children of Sarayaku,
with the wish that they continue to discover the jungle in freedom
—V. J.

Published by Charlesbridge
9 Galen Street
Watertown, MA 02472
(617) 926-0329
www.charlesbridge.com

Library of Congress Cataloging-in-Publication Data
Names: Gualinga, Patricia, author. | Resau, Laura, author. | Jaramillo, Vanessa, illustrator.
Title: Stand as tall as the trees: how an Amazonian community protected the rain forest / Patricia Gualinga
    and Laura Resau; illustrated by Vanessa Jaramillo.
Description: Watertown, MA: Charlesbridge Publishing, 2023. | Includes bibliographical references.|
    Audience: Ages 6–9 | Audience: Grades 2–3 | Summary: "One activist's story shows how Indigenous
    communities can fight to protect their sacred lands—and win."—Provided by publisher.
Identifiers: LCCN 2021053656 (print) | LCCN 2021053657 (ebook) | ISBN 9781623542368 (hardcover) |
    ISBN 9781632895967 (ebook)
Subjects: LCSH: Rain forest conservation—Amazon River Region—Juvenile literature. | Indians of South
    America—Amazon River Region—Juvenile literature. | Environmental protection—Amazon River
    Region—Juvenile literature.
Classification: LCC SD414.A4 G83 2023 (print) | LCC SD414.A4 (ebook) |
    DDC 333.75/16098616--dc23/eng/20211108
LC record available at https://lccn.loc.gov/2021053656
LC ebook record available at https://lccn.loc.gov/2021053657

Printed in China
(hc) 10 9 8 7 6 5 4 3 2 1

Illustrations done in watercolor on paper
Display type set in Blend Caps by Sabrina Mariela Lopez
Text type set in Cheltenham Condensed by Tony Stan
Printed by 1010 Printing International Limited in Huizhou, Guangdong, China
Production supervision by Jennifer Most Delaney
Designed by Kristen Nobles